Water, Water Everywhere!

Ponds

Diyan Leake

Raintree is an imprint of Capstone Global Library Limited, a company incorporated in England and Wales having its registered office at 7 Pilgrim Street, London, EC4V 6LB – Registered company number: 6695582

www.raintreepublishers.co.uk
myorders@raintreepublishers.co.uk

Text © Capstone Global Library Limited 2015
First published in hardback in 2014
Paperback edition first published in 2015
The moral rights of the proprietor have been asserted.

Edited by Joanna Issa and Penny West
Designed by Philippa Jenkins
Original illustrations © Capstone Global Library Ltd 2014
Picture research by Mica Brancic
Production by Helen McCreath
Originated by Capstone Global Library Ltd
Printed and bound in China

ISBN 978 1 406 28389 1 (hardback)
18 17 16 15 14
10 9 8 7 6 5 4 3 2 1

ISBN 978 1 406 28395 2 (paperback)
19 18 17 16 15
10 9 8 7 6 5 4 3 2 1

British Library Cataloguing in Publication Data
Leake, Diyan
        Ponds (Water, Water Everywhere!)
A full catalogue record for this book is available from the British Library.

Acknowledgements
We would like to thank the following for permission to reproduce photographs: Alamy pp. 4 (© Arco Images GmbH). 5, 23c (© Tom Grundy), 8 (© The Photolibrary Wales/Steve Benbow), 10 (© blickwinkel), 11, 22a (© Paul Thompson Images), 16 (© Kelly-marie smith), 17 (© Nicholas Toh), 18 (© Andrew Horner), 19, 23b (© Cristina Lichti), 20 (© Image Source Plus); Corbis p. 21 (Blend Images/© Hill Street Studios); FLPA pp. 9 (Minden Pictures/Gerry Ellis), 13 (Malcolm Schuyl); Getty Images pp. 6, 23a (Stone+/Diane Cook and Len Jenshel); Shutterstock pp. 7 (© Matt Gibson), 12 (© Wang LiQiang), 14 (© Alexander Potapov), 15 (© Paladin12), 22b (© Waynelmage), 22c (© windu).

Cover photograph reproduced with permission of Shutterstock (© Tessa Bishop).
Back cover photograph reproduced with permission of Shutterstock/© Alexander Potapov.

We would like to thank Michael Bright and Diana Bentley for their invaluable help in the preparation of this book.

Every effort has been made to contact copyright holders of material reproduced in this book. Any omissions will be rectified in subsequent printings if notice is given to the publisher.

All the Internet addresses (URLs) given in this book were valid at the time of going to press. However, due to the dynamic nature of the Internet, some addresses may have changed, or sites may have changed or ceased to exist since publication. While the author and publisher regret any inconvenience this may cause readers, no responsibility for any such changes can be accepted by either the author or the publisher.

Contents

Ponds

A pond is a body of water.

A pond has shallow water.

A pond is like a small lake.

A pond has land all around it.

What makes a pond?

Some ponds are made by nature.

Beavers made this pond using
tree branches.

Some ponds are made by people.

Some people like to have a
pond in their garden.

Animals in ponds

Some birds live in ponds.

Some snails live in ponds.

Frogs live in ponds.

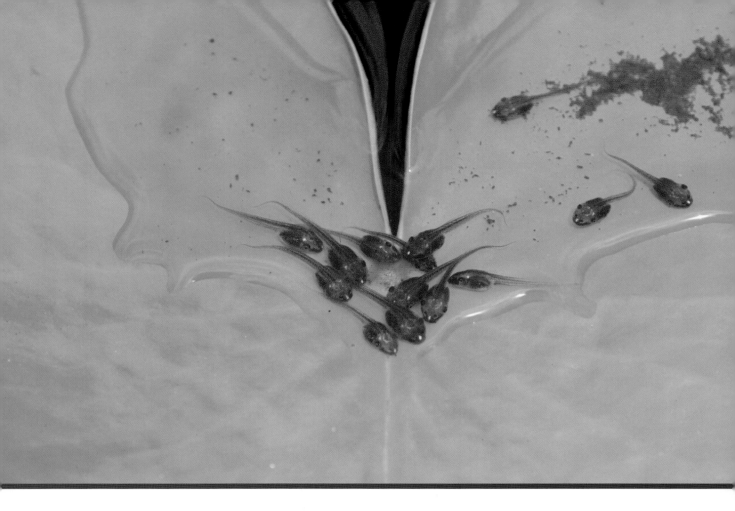

Tadpoles live in ponds.

Some insects live near ponds.

This insect can walk on the water.

Plants in ponds

Plants live in ponds.

rushes

This duck has made a nest out of rushes.

Having fun by ponds

It is fun to spend time by a pond.

Stay safe! Always have an adult with you when you are near water.

Quiz

Which of these is a pond?

A

B

C

Answer on page 24

Picture glossary

nature everything in the world not made by people or machines

rushes stiff plants that grow in water or on very wet land

shallow not deep

Index

Answer to quiz on page 22: Picture **A** shows a pond.

Note to parents and teachers
Before reading
Show the children the photograph on the cover of the book. Can they say what sort of water the photograph shows? Can they name some of the animals that might live there? Have they ever seen a pond? What did they do while they were there? Do any of them have a pond in their garden?

After reading
- Plan a pond-dipping trip with the children. Before you go on your trip, ask them to draw the animals and plants they would expect to see in or around the pond. Show them pictures of animals and plants that are common in your area.
- Show the children the picture of tadpoles on page 15 again. Ask them if they know what animal a tadpole grows into. Use cut-outs of the different life stages of a frog to talk about how a tadpole changes.